# THE VINEYARD BOOK

JACK JOHNSTON          ART: MOIRA MANION

ISBN          0-9629880-0-6

ISBN-13  978-0-9629880-0-4


Library of Congress Control Number: 2004097286


First Printing October 2005


Published by ACME PRESS

1116 E Deep Run Rd, PO Box 1702

Westminster, Md 21158


Printed in China by South China Printing


10 9 8 7 6 5 4 3 2 1

# THE VINEYARD BOOK

ACME PRESS
PO BOX 1702
WESTMINSTER, MD 21158

JACK JOHNSTON          ART: MOIRA MANION

Way out in the country, there is a farm.

It has a barn with tractors, mowers, wagons and sprayers.

It has a pond with fish, frogs and sometimes ducks and geese.

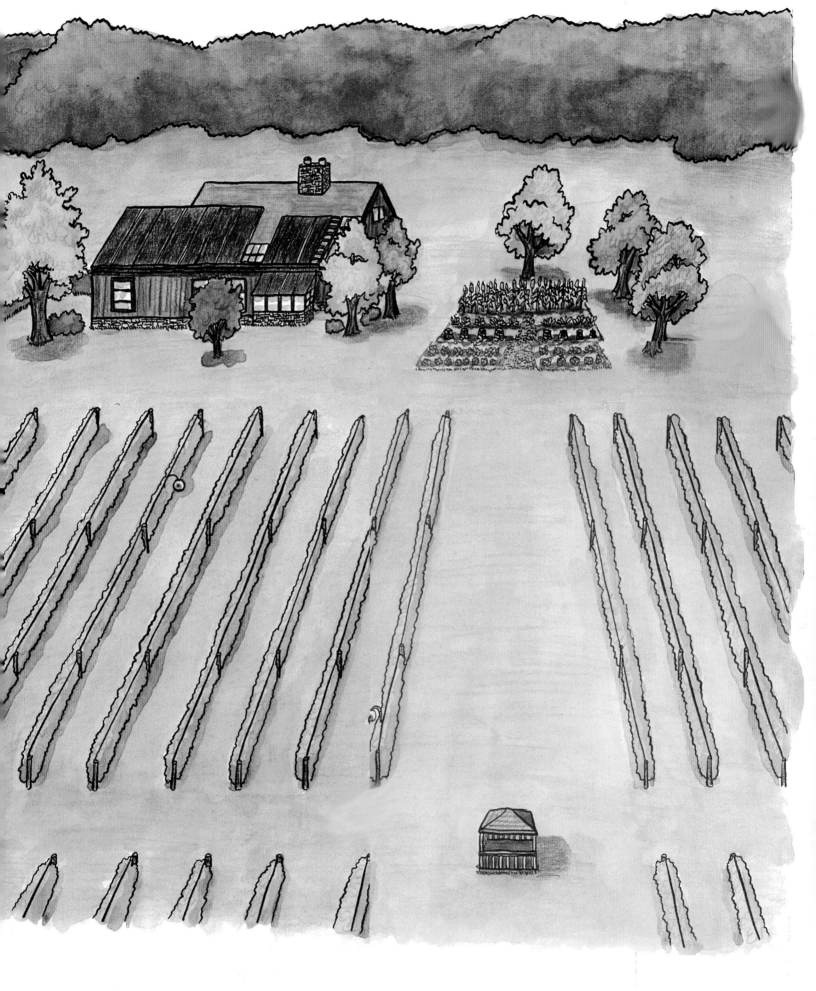

It has a garden with vegetables, herbs and too many rocks.

It has some woods with squirrels, deer and lots of noisy birds.

And it has a big VINEYARD where grapes are grown.

It is called COPERNICA VINEYARDS.
It is named after Nicolaus Copernicus,
who discovered that the sun is the center
of our solar system. That means all the
planets revolve around the sun.

Life on this farm revolves around the vineyard.
That means the vineyard is the center of life here on the farm,
and the vines depend very much on the sun for growth and health.

There are FIVE THOUSAND grapevines in the vineyard.
Each year, the grapes are picked and sold to several wineries who
crush them and press out the juice to make fine wines.

The grapes are picked . . .

. . . crushed . . .

. . . pressed . . .

. . . and made into wine.

You need lots of equipment to manage a vineyard.

You need a big tractor. It has to have lots of power to pull heavy equipment and get you through the mud and rough spots.

You have to have a sprayer, to spray the harmful insects on the vines, and to prevent diseases. The sprayer is pulled by the tractor.

You need a wagon to haul the grapes from the vineyard after they've been picked. The wagon is also pulled by the tractor.

You need a mower to cut the grass and weeds in the vineyard. Some mowers have several sharp blades underneath which cut a wide swath.

Others, like this Bush Hog, have one BIG blade which can cut down almost anything in its path.

You need some pruning shears to trim the vines and cut off the clusters of grapes when they are ripe.

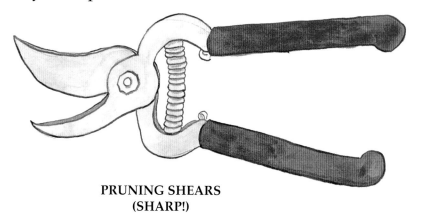

**PRUNING SHEARS
(SHARP!)**

**A PRUNE
(THESE ARE FOR EATING,
NOT CUTTING)**

You need gloves to protect your hands, and a hat to protect your head from the sun on hot days.

**GLOVES (SIZE M)**

**HAT (SIZE L)**

You need some plastic ties to fasten the vines to the trellis wire so they don't break in a strong wind, or sag down onto the ground where the grapes might rot.

You need lots of strong plastic buckets called LUGS to put the grapes in as they are being picked.

A LUG

LUGGING
A LUG

There are some other things that aren't really necessary, but are nice to have just the same.

One is a golf cart—not for playing golf, but to carry tools and equipment around in the vineyard.

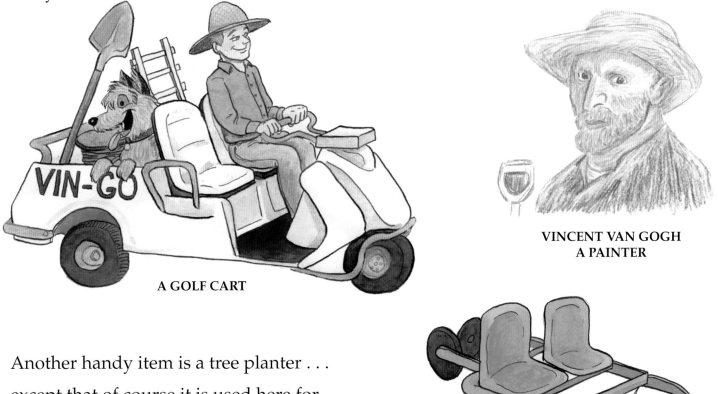

VIN-GO

A GOLF CART

VINCENT VAN GOGH
A PAINTER

Another handy item is a tree planter . . . except that of course it is used here for planting vines, not trees.

The planter is attached to the back of the tractor, and has a V-shaped plow in front that digs a deep trench as it is pulled along. Two people can ride in the planter and plant the vines in the trench.

It's always nice to have some rose bushes at the end of each row of vines. They aren't necessary, but they add lots of color.

But the most important item of all . . . you need a couple of faithful vineyard helpers to make sure you do everything right.

Copernica Vineyards has two vineyard helpers:

Truman Capuddy . . .

. . . and Oliver.

Truman helps by
standing on your foot . . .

. . . by sharpening his
claws on a grapevine trunk . . .

. . . and by attacking any
loose grapevine branches.

Oliver helps by chasing Truman . . .

. . . although sometimes it's the other way around.

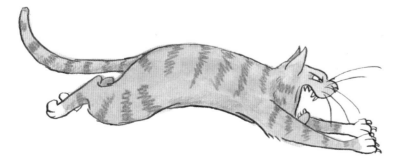

How does a vineyard get started?

You have to plant it, just like you do a garden.

Except that you don't start with seeds—you plant CUTTINGS.

One way to do this is to cut pieces from older vines and put

them into pots where they grow roots of their own.

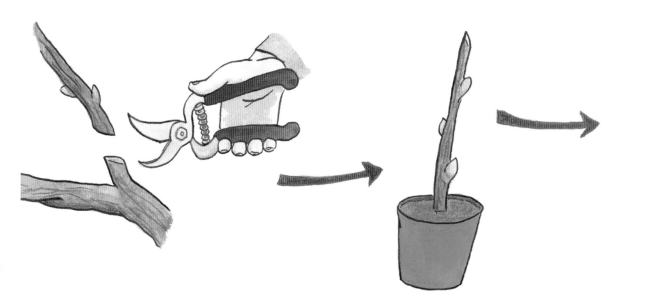

To make the vine grow better, it is often necessary to join pieces
from two different kinds of vines. This is called GRAFTING.

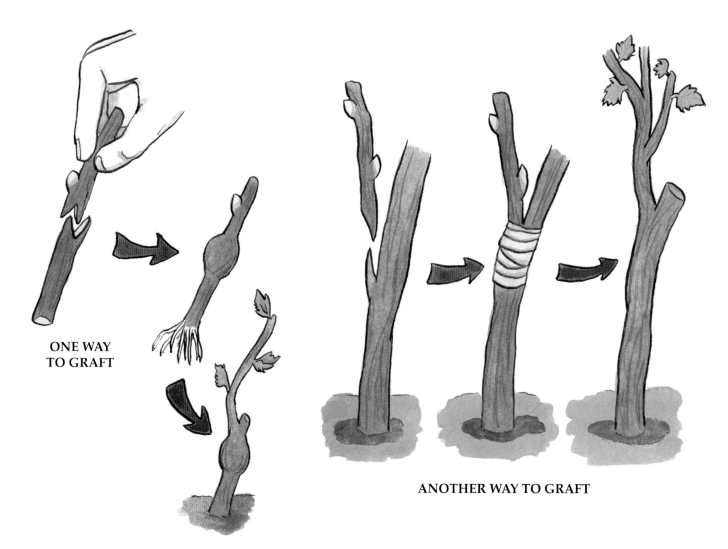

**ONE WAY
TO GRAFT**

**ANOTHER WAY TO GRAFT**

Once you decide where the vineyard
is to be, the first step is to give
the ground a thorough plowing,
to loosen the soil . . .

. . . and a disking to
smooth it out.

If you don't have many vines to plant,
you can just dig a hole for each one . . .

. . . stick the rooted ends of
the vines into the holes,
and cover them up.

A stake is driven into
the ground next to each
one so the vines will grow
up straight.

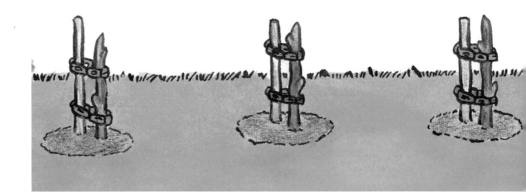

Some people prefer to put
plastic tubes around the
vines for support and to
protect them from damage.

But if you have lots of vines, then it's easier to use a tree planter.

Two people ride on the planter. As the tractor moves down the row, digging a trench, one person dips a cutting into a bucket of some goopy mess which keeps the roots wet, then hands it to the other person, who places it straight up in the trench.

It helps if both people are the same size, or the trench will be lopsided.

The next step is to put in the trellis posts. These will hold the wires which support the vines when they are grown. If the vineyard is small, you can use a post-hole digger to dig the holes for the posts.

But this is a lot of work. The job will go much faster with a big drill which attaches to the rear of the tractor.

If the ground is hard or
full of rocks, even a
driller can have problems.

And you have to be
careful not to drill
too deep or the driller
can get stuck.

When all the holes are dug, a heavy wooden post is placed in each one. Then dirt and rocks are packed around them to make sure they all fit tight.

Next you have to attach heavy wire along the rows, fastening it to each of the posts. The wire comes in long rolls and has to be unwound carefully, or it will get all tangled up.

The best way to do this is to use a SPINNING JENNY . . .

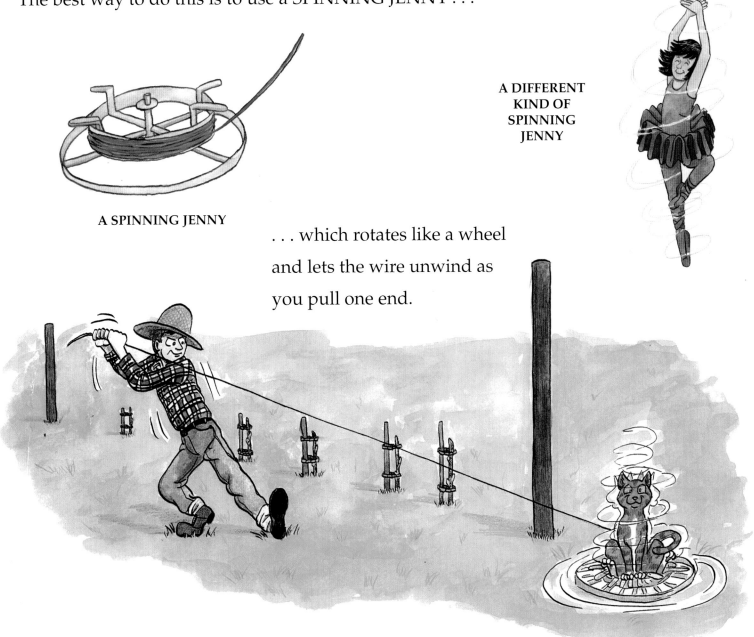

**A SPINNING JENNY**

**A DIFFERENT KIND OF SPINNING JENNY**

. . . which rotates like a wheel and lets the wire unwind as you pull one end.

After this is done, you have to do it all over again, because vines need at least TWO wires . . .

one up high . . .

. . . and one down low.

Now that the vines are planted, the next thing to do is . . . WAIT . . .

. . . and WAIT . . .

. . . and WAIT . . .

In fact, you have to wait TWO YEARS, because it takes that long for vines to get big and strong enough to start making grapes.

During that time, you have to TRAIN the vines, to make sure they grow the way you want them to. The simplest way to do this is to let two arms grow out from the trunks along the lower wire.

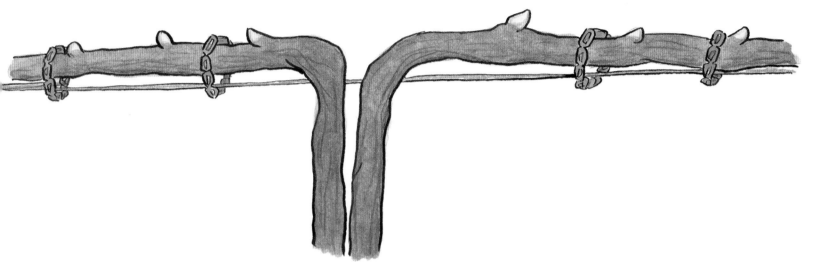

The arms are called CORDONS, and they contain lots of buds.

Things start growing in the spring. The buds start to swell, and pretty soon a tiny shoot with delicate green leaves emerges from each one.

Each day, the shoots grow higher and higher, making more leaves, until they reach the top wire. And soon something that looks like tiny bunches of grapes appears.

They are not really grapes, however—they are clusters of little buds from which flower blossoms will burst a few weeks later.

It is these flowers that produce the baby grapes, which grow together in little bunches. They are green in color, and very hard.

During the summer, the bunches of grapes get bigger and bigger as the shoots grow taller and taller . . . until finally the grapes start to soften and change color.

In France, this time is called VERAISON. We don't have a word for it in English, so we just use the French word. It is pronounced VERY-*ZON* (or something like that).

Some of the grapes turn golden, or straw-colored. These are used to make white wine . . . which isn't really white at all.

Others turn dark blue or purple. These are used to make red wine . . . which isn't really red at all. Does that make any sense to you?

Now, it would be nice if all these things happened without any problems. But unfortunately, there are lots of things that can go wrong . . . and usually do!

First, there are BUGS that think all parts of grapevines are simply DELICIOUS.

There are insects that chew on the roots . . .

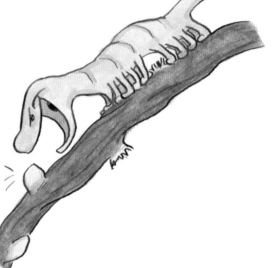

. . . and there are worms that eat the tiny buds . . .

. . . and there are beetles that eat the leaves.

Besides the bugs, there are lots of DISEASES that can damage the fruit. Grapevines can get sick, just like people.

These diseases have ugly names, like BLACK ROT and POWDERY MILDEW, and this is what they do to the grapes. . . .

Regular and careful spraying will kill the bugs and prevent most of the diseases. So before they have a chance to damage the vines, it's time to hook up the sprayer.

Special materials to fight the bugs and diseases are mixed with water in the spray tank . . .

The tractor pulls the sprayer up and down the rows of the vineyard, where it blows big clouds of spray onto the vines.

Unfortunately, some of the bugs and diseases keep coming back all during the growing season—which means we'll be needing the sprayer again and again, until late in the summer when all the dangers are past.

There are problems with this.
You can't spray on a rainy day . . .

. . . or on a windy day . . .

. . . or when the tractor or sprayer breaks down . . . which always seems to happen just when you need them the most.

Weeds are another problem. They grow fast, and if you're not careful they can overtake a vineyard.

Spraying the weeds, like you sprayed the bugs, gets rid of them. But you have to be careful, because some sprays can damage the vines as well as the weeds.

Planting grass between the rows helps to keep the weeds down. But then you have to mow the grass . . . another job for the tractor.

Another solution to the weed problem is to plow them up. There is a special gadget for just this sort of thing. It fastens onto the side of the tractor and churns up the ground as the tractor drives along the row.

You have to be careful with this plow, however, because if you get too close to the vines . . .

There are still more problems which can affect the vineyard. Some of those nice animals who live in and around the woods like to EAT the grapes, and often do a lot of damage.

You can't spray them, or mow them, so about all you can do is keep them out of the vineyard.

A fence works pretty well, but it's expensive.

Some people put up
scarecrows to keep
deer away, but the deer
aren't easily fooled.

Some people hang soap or bags of hair-cuttings around the vines, because some
animals don't like the smell. But if they're hungry enough, they'll just hold their noses.

Birds are the biggest problem. A big flock of hungry robins or starlings can strip a vineyard bare in a few hours.

To keep birds away, some people hang balloons with big eyes painted on them. They do scare some birds, but you have to keep moving them around or the birds will get used to them.

Another method is FLASH TAPE, which is a long shiny ribbon that is stretched above the vines. The wind causes it to twist and reflect the light, and this also scares the birds.

There are machines that make loud noises, like cannons, and some that imitate the distress cries of birds. These work very well, but neighbors don't like them much.

Some people spray hot pepper sauce on the grapes, which burns the birds' tongues. It can burn people tongues too, if you accidentally get some in your mouth.

The best method is to put big nets over the vines to keep the birds from getting to the grapes. But it is also very expensive and very difficult to put up and take down.

If the vineyard survives all these problems, the grapes will get very sweet, and soon it will be time to pick them.

How do you know exactly when they are ready to pick? One way is to squeeze the juice out of some grapes from different parts of the vineyard and put it in a glass tube . . .

Then a special glass measuring rod is dropped into the juice. The sweeter the grapes, the higher the rod will float in the tube. When it floats high enough, the grapes are ripe enough to pick.

Which means that it's HARVEST TIME! Everybody gets excited because this is the BIG moment of the year!

Some vineyards have giant machines which actually drive over the tops of the rows and shake the grapes off the vines. These machines are very expensive and are used only in very large vineyards.

At Copernica Vineyards, the grapes are picked by hand. Lots of hands, actually. It takes 30 or 40 people almost two whole days to do the job.

In addition to lots of pickers,
you need lots of lugs . . .

. . . scales to weigh the lugs when
they are full . . .

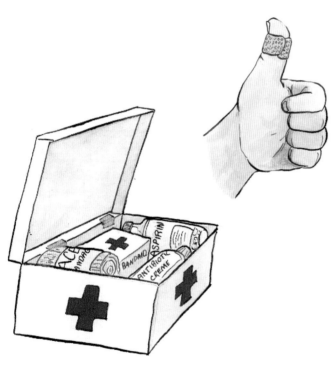

. . . a first aid kit, in case someone cuts
a finger or gets stung by a bee . . .

. . . and, perhaps most important,
GOOD WEATHER. No one likes to
pick grapes in the rain!

As the lugs are filled with grapes, they are loaded onto a wagon and taken to the scales to be weighed.

Wineries which buy the grapes pay for them by the pound, so it's important to know how much everything weighs. All the grapes picked each year at Copernica Vineyards weigh THIRTY THOUSAND POUNDS! That's 15 TONS . . .

as much as 3 ELEPHANTS . . .

. . . or an ARMY TANK!

The lugs are then stacked onto a truck for delivery. The truck will have to make several trips, because that's too much to carry all at once.

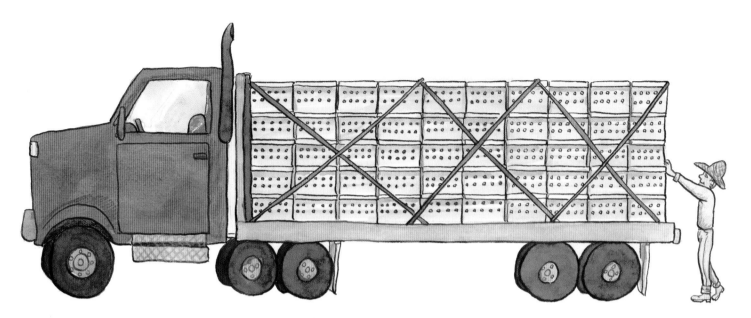

When all the grapes have been picked, everybody celebrates with a picnic, with lots of good things to eat and drink. Another harvest is over at last!

But the work isn't finished yet. In fact, one of the most important tasks is still to come . . .

As winter approaches, and the vines drop their leaves, the vineyard looks like this:

If it were left that way, here's what it would look like next season:

So we have to PRUNE the vines—that means cutting off most of the old growth so that the vines can get a fresh start in the spring. Just enough buds are left to make new shoots which will produce next year's crop of grapes.

Pruning takes a long time—most of the winter, in fact. And those freezing temperatures don't make the job any easier!

Sometimes part of a vine has gotten diseased or damaged. So instead of cutting off all its old shoots, one or more are used to replace the damaged ones.

When the pruning is finally finished, the vineyard looks pretty much the way it did last spring.

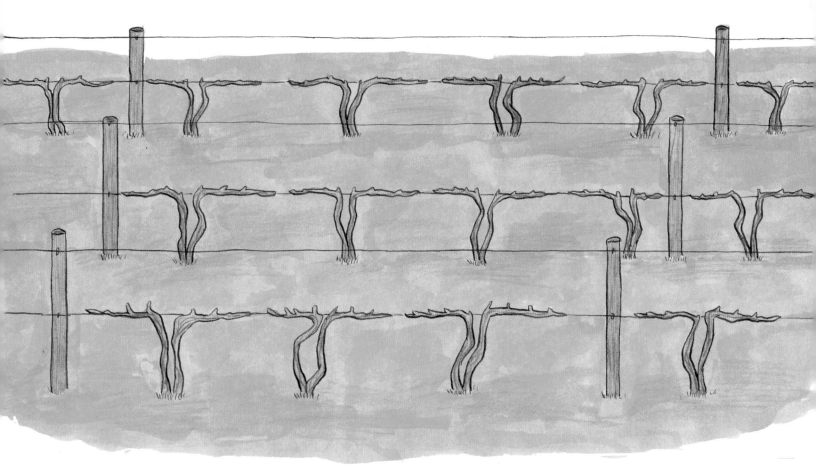

Spring arrives, and there's still one more job to do before the vines start to grow again.

All the equipment which will be needed in the coming season—the tractor, the wagon, the sprayer—must be ready to do their jobs. They have to be cleaned up, oiled, greased, and checked for problems.

Everything must be ready to go when the time comes.

And when the time does come, the whole vineyard adventure starts all over again.